An Irish Tales Book

Brokaw Enterprises LLC
Chicago, IL

www.irishtalesonline.com
customerservice@irishtalesonline.com

Text by Paul Kostolansky
Illustrations by Greg Broyles

The university names and logos featured in this book are registered trademarks of that university.

"Play Like A Champion Today" is used courtesy of PLACT, Inc.

"Chicken Soup" is used in the title of this book with permission of Chicken Soup for the Soul Enterprises, Inc.

Photo credits: cover, Louis Hill; illustration #19, Notre Dame Archives; illustrations #2, #20, and #22, South Bend Tribune

Manufactured in the United States
First Edition
2005

Library of Congress Control Number: 2005907235

ISBN 0-9772021-0-0

Thanks to everyone who helped along the way, including Annie Weed, Tomi Gerhold, Sara Liebscher, Vanessa Cox, Charles Lamb, Charlie Fiss, Rick Poulter, Louis Hill and the Notre Dame players, coaches and/or their families who graciously chose to participate in the project. And last but not least, a very special thanks to Megan and Katy for their Notre Dame artwork.

On January 1, 1979, in the Cotton Bowl Classic against the University of Houston, Notre Dame completed one of the greatest comeback victories in college football history. It took the effort of every player and coach to make that happen. Admittedly, in the cold and icy weather, when we trailed by 22 points with less than eight minutes left in the fourth quarter, the game seemed hopeless. In fact, believing that the Cotton Bowl game had already been decided, millions of people across America turned off their television sets or switched the channel to another game. But we never gave up and neither did our loyal fans. We continued playing hard, trying to create the play that would turn the game around, and eventually we succeeded. The game only lasted sixty minutes, but the lessons learned and the friendships made on that cold Dallas afternoon continue on in the lives of all the Notre Dame family who witnessed the miraculous comeback. I hope you enjoy the game as retold in the following pages as much as we did over twenty five years ago. And remember, never give up in the pursuit of your dreams!

Joe Unis
#99

THE CHICKEN SOUP GAME

1979 COTTON BOWL

NOTRE DAME FIGHTING IRISH
VS
HOUSTON COUGARS

An Irish Tales Book

Brokaw Enterprises LLC
Chicago, IL

In 1979, on New Year's Day, the Notre Dame Fighting Irish football team was in Dallas, Texas to play in the Cotton Bowl. It was the fourth time Notre Dame played in the Bowl. It was also the second year in a row.

The year before, Notre Dame beat the Texas Longhorns to win their tenth National Championship. This time, Notre Dame would face the Houston Cougars and their complicated option offense.

It was bitter cold and windy in Dallas that day.
So cold in fact, that the seats in the stadium had
icicles on them. Only half of the 72,000 people who
bought tickets went to the game.

At the start of the football season, Notre Dame was the fifth best team in the country. The Irish won eight games and lost three that year. In the very last game, Notre Dame lost to the Southern California Trojans on the last play. The Trojans were the Irish's fiercest rival and the Irish were disappointed to lose. Notre Dame's Head Coach Dan Devine had the Irish ready to play in the Cotton Bowl though.

The Houston Cougars finished the season with nine wins and two losses. Two of the wins were against the Texas Longhorns and the Texas A&M Aggies. These wins helped the Cougars win the Southwest Conference that year.

After the game started, both teams had trouble scoring because of the cold weather. Notre Dame took advantage of a Houston fumble to score the game's first touchdown. A second Houston fumble was recovered by freshman and future All-American Bob Crable. This led to another touchdown. Notre Dame's extra point and two-point conversion attempts failed, and the Irish now led 12-0.

The momentum soon shifted as the Cougars scored after four straight Irish turnovers! The Cougars scored two touchdowns and then kicked two field goals. This gave them a 20-12 halftime lead.

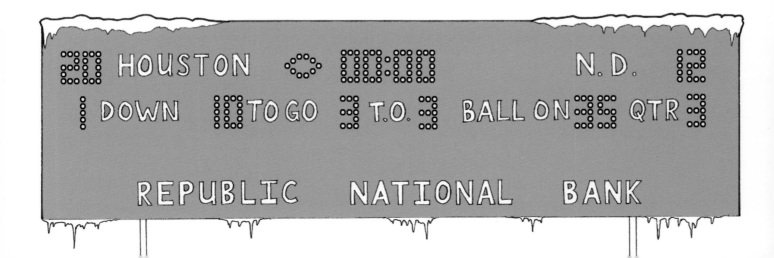

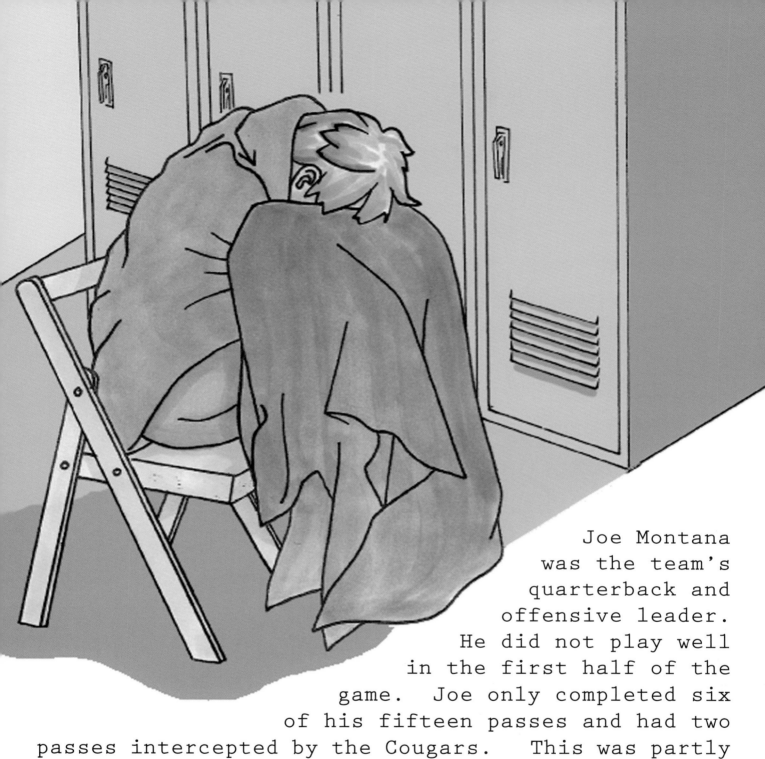

Joe Montana
was the team's
quarterback and
offensive leader.
He did not play well
in the first half of the
game. Joe only completed six
of his fifteen passes and had two
passes intercepted by the Cougars. This was partly
because Joe was feeling sick before the game.
Sitting in the locker room at halftime, Joe now
felt sicker. He started shivering and his body
temperature dropped below normal. The team was
told that Joe could not play anymore that day.

When Irish Center Dave Huffman heard this, he said
"we thought it was over."

Notre Dame's team doctor, Les Bodnar, had an idea though. He stayed in the locker room with Joe after the second half of the game started and made him a cup of chicken soup.

Joe ate the soup and his body temperature returned to normal. Joe started to feel better. So much better that he went back out to play late in the third quarter.

Seeing Joe return gave the Irish hope, but the team's situation only grew worse. Joe only completed one of his first eleven passes. He also threw his third interception. Safety Joe Restic and Linebacker Bob Golic, the team's defensive leaders, were also lost to injuries.

Houston scored two more touchdowns and now led the Irish 34-12. All hopes of an Irish victory had vanished.

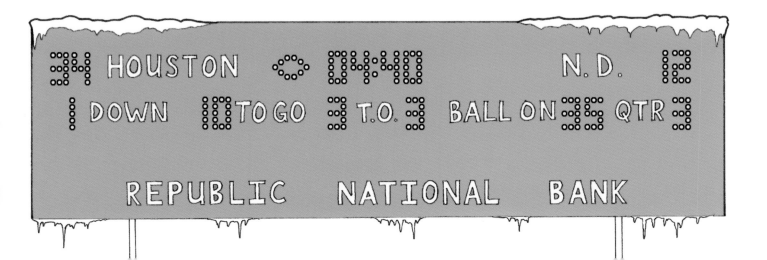

34 HOUSTON   N.D. 12

1 DOWN   10 TO GO   3 T.O. 3   BALL ON   QTR

REPUBLIC NATIONAL BANK

The Irish's
luck
changed
with
7 minutes
and 35 seconds
left
in the game.
Notre Dame
player
Tony Belden
blocked
a Houston
punt.

His teammate Steve Cichy returned the ball 33 yards for a touchdown. The two-point conversion was good. The Irish now only trailed 34-20.

The Irish defense stopped the Cougars the next time they had the ball. The Irish offense then moved 61 yards in five plays for another touchdown. A great catch by running back Jerome Heavens set up the score. The two-point conversion attempt was again good. Now the Irish only trailed 34-28 with 4 minutes and 15 seconds
left in
the game.

The Irish got the ball back quickly but this time Joe fumbled at the Houston twenty yard line! The Irish defense stiffened and forced the Cougars into a fourth down. Houston needed one yard for a first down. They decided to go for it instead of punting into a stiff wind.

Houston ran the ball up the middle. Irish players Joe Gramke and Mike Calhoun made "The Hit" and stopped the Houston running back for no gain! Notre Dame would get the ball back. They had one more chance to win the game.

There were only 28 seconds left in the game. Joe scrambled for one first down. He then threw to his go-to receiver Kris Haines for another. The ball was now on the Houston eight yard line. There were only 6 seconds left.

Irish head coach Dan Devine called a time out to talk to Joe. Coach Devine decided
to run two quick plays
instead of one
long one.

The first was called "91", a quick "out" pattern by both wide receivers.

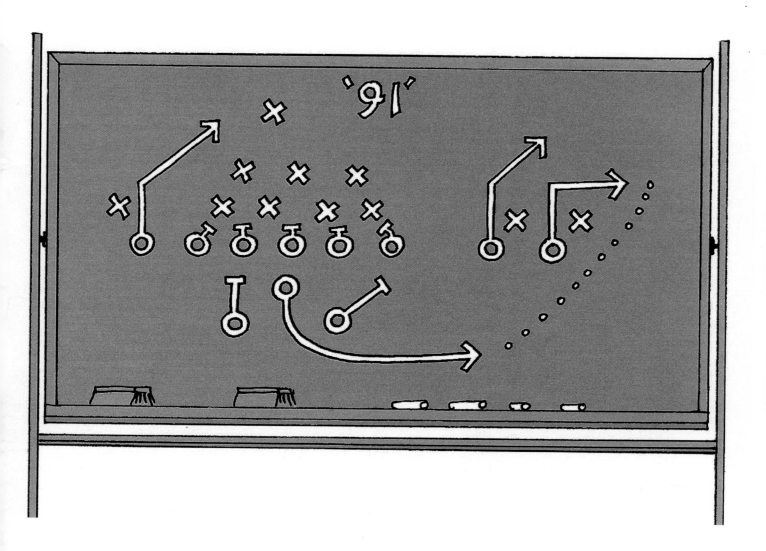

Kris Haines was not open on the play so Joe threw the ball away. Only 2 seconds left. There was time for one more play.

In the huddle before the last play, Joe asked Kris "can you beat your man?" Kris said "yes". So Joe called the same play again.

The Irish lined up for the last time that day. Joe
took the snap and ran to his right as time ran out.
Joe threw to Kris who was diving in the front corner
of the end zone.

"And it's a touchdown, a touchdown taken at the corner!" yelled Lindsey Nelson, the game's play-by-play announcer. Kris had caught the pass. The Irish had tied the score with no time left in the game!

Notre Dame's
      sideline
            erupted in
                  jubilation!

The Irish had not won yet though. Joe Unis, the
Irish's kicker, had to kick the extra point.

The ball was snapped.
The kick was up.

It was good!

But wait!

There was a
penalty against
the Irish.

They would have
to kick the extra
point again, and
from five yards
further away.

The Irish lined up for the second extra point attempt. The ball was snapped. The Cougars rushed every player and nearly blocked the kick!

Joe got the kick off and it sailed through the goal posts. The kick was good and the Irish victory was now complete!

Notre Dame had come back from a 22-point deficit in less than 8 minutes. The game was the 600th victory for the Notre Dame football program. It was also one of the greatest comebacks in the history of college football. And with the help of a little chicken soup, it solidified Joe Montana's reputation as "The Comeback Kid."

The End

For Mom and Dad

GAME SUMMARY

	1Q	2Q	3Q	4Q	FINAL
NOTRE DAME	12	0	0	23	35
HOUSTON	7	13	14	0	34

FIRST QUARTER
NOTRE DAME - Joe Montana 3 yard run (Joe Unis kick failed); @6:55, 66 yards in 9 plays following fumble recovery by Jay Case
NOTRE DAME - Buchanan 1 yard run (Montana pass failed); @4:40, 25 yards in 6 plays following fumble recovery by Bob Crable
HOUSTON - Willis Adams 15 yard pass from Danny Davis (Kenny Hatfield kick); @0:17, 12 yards in 3 plays following fumble recovery by Chuck Brown

SECOND QUARTER
HOUSTON - Randy Love 1 yard run (Hatfield kick); @6:27, 21 yards in 6 plays following fumble recovery by David Hodge
HOUSTON - Hatfield 21 yard FG; @3:00, 21 yards in 6 plays following interception by Hatfield

HOUSTON - Hatfield 34 yard FG; @0:03, 39 yards in 7 plays following interception by Steve Bradham

THIRD QUARTER
HOUSTON - Davis 2 yard run (Hatfield kick); @6:29, 38 yards in 8 plays following punt
HOUSTON - Davis 5 yard run (Hatfield kick); @4:40, 19 yards in 3 plays following blocked punt by Bobby Harrison

FOURTH QUARTER
NOTRE DAME - Steve Cichy 33 yard return of blocked punt (Vagas Ferguson pass from Montana); @7:25, following blocked punt by Tony Belden
NOTRE DAME - Montana 2 yard run (Kris Haines pass from Montana); @4:15, 61 yards in 5 plays following punt
NOTRE DAME - Haines 8 yard pass from Montana (Unis kick); @0:00, 29 yards in 4 plays after taking over on downs

GAME STATISTICS

TEAM STATS	ND	UH
First Downs	13	16
Rushing	4	12
Passing	7	3
Penalty	2	1
Rushes - Net Yards	40-131	63-229
Net Yards Passing	163	60
Passes	13-37-4	4-13-0
Total Plays	77	76
Total Net Yards	294	289
Fumbles - Lost	3-3	6-3
Penalties - Yards	8-74	6-39
Punts - Average	7-26	10-26

INDIVIDUAL STATS
RUSHING - NOTRE DAME: Heavens 16-71, Montana 7-26, Ferguson 10-19, Pallas 4-11, Mitchell 1-3, Buchanan 2-1; HOUSTON: Davis 19-76, King 21-73, Love 22-73, Brown 1-6

PASSING - NOTRE DAME: Montana 13-34-4 (163 yards), Koegel 0-3-0; HOUSTON: Davis 4-12-0 (60 yards), Brown 0-1-0

RECEIVING - NOTRE DAME: Heavens 4-60, Haines 4-31, Masztak 3-49, Holohan 1-14, Ferguson 1-9; HOUSTON: Adams 2-35, Herring 2-25

PUNTING - NOTRE DAME: Boushka 4-34, Restic 2-25, team 1-0; HOUSTON: Wyatt 8-32, team 2-0

Look for new Irish Tales books about other great Irish games soon!

I ♥ Notre Dame

N D